# My Today's Thirty Days Affirmations

ISBN: 979-8-218-14960-4

Proofread by: Julie P Emming
Editor: Adam Havens

I would like to dedicate this book to my mother Fadiah Mujib who has been by my side from day 1.
I would also like to dedicate this book to my father Abdus-Shakur Abdul-Mujib. May God grant you paradise.
My kids Yasmine, Kiara, Khyree & Spencer.

I would like to thank First Step Recovery Center who gave me the inspiration to write this book.

A special thanks goes to Christina Parker.
I would also like to thank a special friend Kari Kennedy
Mr. Derrick, Ms. Courtney, Ms. Kelly, Victoria, Ms. Caroline, James, Donna, Julie, Adam, Kyle,

Kaylyn, Erin, Brittany & the rest of
the First Step staff.

# DAY 1

Today, I will not make excuses. Nor will I waste my time and energy on my past actions because yesterday is gone while today is all that I have and tomorrow is not promised. Today, I will not allow the negativity of my past to define the person that I am today. Surely Today, I am that positive person who will shine forth through tomorrow!

# DAY 2

Today, I will count my blessings, because I am blessed to be breathing. Today, I will be thankful as well as grateful for the things that I have. Today, I will remove all limits on my life that will stop me from growing spiritually, mentally, emotionally as well as physically. Today, I will chase my dreams. Knowing that I can accomplish any and everything I choose to accomplish. I will not settle for less, knowing that I can be the best!

# Day 3

Today. I will commit to being a leader and not a follower. Today, I will lead myself away from the pain and misery that has been a dark cloud over my life. Today, I will continue to make those much-needed sacrifices in my life so that all my dreams May come true. Today, I have a great opportunity to do whatever I choose to do!

# Day 4

Today, I will take full responsibility for my past actions by realizing that I am the reason that everything in my past, was the result of my own actions so today step-by-step through my actions and hard work with full dedication I will grow into that person I want to be I will become that person through good character!

# Day 5

Today, I will not tiptoe to accomplishing my goals but run to my goals. Today, I will find a way when there is no way. Today, I will keep doing the right things in life when others are doing the wrong things. Today, I cannot stop, nor will I be stopped!

# Day 6

Today, I will be consistent in staying positive and putting in that much needed hard work so that I can be successful. Today, I will validate myself, and not put the blame on anyone else. Today, I know that my life is whatever I make it!

# Day 7

Today, I claim the light that shines over all to become the sun, which is only a gang of stars. Today, wherever there is darkness, there shall be none of me. Today, I will move with the positive forces of energy in life!

# Day 8

Today, I will give more value to my life by being selfless, and not selfish. Today, I will volunteer my time to help the next person, so I may produce a long, lasting relationship with selflessness. Today, I will not act out of pride but act out from my heart!

# Day 9

Today, I will thrive for success so that tomorrow, I will live in success for success is built with hard work, blood, sweat and tears. Today, my quality of being will be of good nature.

# Day 10

Today, I realize that everything that I need to know is contained within for there within is an angel called self, who shall reveal itself unto me when the time is true, then truth, shall reveal itself unto me, but first, I must practice self-control, which is the key to my own existence and my own soul. Today, is a day of discipline. I will discipline myself to control myself to grow myself.

# Day 11

Today, I will separate myself from the naysayers the negative and cynical people. Today, I will remove certain words from my vocabulary, like can't, try, maybe, impossible. Today, I know I can do anything I want to do because anything is possible through the will and the help of the creator. Today, I will speak the right words into existence, so that I may be all that I will become!

# Day 12

Today, I will utilize the most powerful tool in the world, which is my mind. Today, I will concentrate on that which is important. Today, I will focus all my energy on one thing at a time. Today, I will stay aware of that which is a distraction that will drain my energy into confusion. Today, I will transform my energy into a world of progression!

# Day 13

Today, I will own my life. Today, I will invest in me. Today, I will do what I want to do. Today, I will write my vision, so that I may bring forth what I wrote. Today, I will hold myself accountable. Today, I will not be playing. Today I will live for me and not society. Today, I will make myself the happiest person on this planet!

# Day 14

Today, I will treat my life like a butterfly by being rare and gentle. Rare because I am unique, and there is no one like me and gentle because, I only live once, so I must make all the right decisions. Today, I will continue to fly in the right direction!

# Day 15

Today, I will be brave. Today, I will be energized. Today, I will be kind. Today, I will let go of my devilish ways. Today, I will raise myself above the madness of the world. Today, I will not be lonely. Today, I will not be sad. Today, I will live life with all the love of God!

# Day 16

Today, I will not allow no one or nothing to control my life. Today, I will be the power in my life. Today, I will focus on my inner strength so that I may lead myself to the land of happiness. Today, I will manifest all of God that's in me, as well as his blessings to shine forth throughout my life!

# Day 17

Today, I will live with the faith of God instead of the doubts of the devil. Today, I will not live in fear of not seeing the beauty of who I am. Today I will be courageous and confident, in everything that I do!

# Day 18

Today. I will build myself a better life through righteousness and positivity by destroying all my negative thoughts, and negative ways. Today, I will build a civilized life and destroy my uncivilized way of life as I live for better days!

# Day 19

Today, I will not allow my emotions to control my life. Today, I will allow mental stability to be the core of my existence. Today, I will deal with facts and not opinions. Today, I will truly believe in myself by executing all that which I have learned.

# Day 20

Today, I know, I Live to die only to live again. Today, I will live life as a traveler striving through Time and, space, utilizing all that is good, and staying away from all that is evil. Today, I will be amazed with myself, because nobody does me better than I do me!

# Day 21

Today, I will live for the ups and prepare for the downs. Today, I know that God puts no burden on no soul that it can't handle, Today, I know that all obstacles that are in my life are just Boot Camp for success!

# Day 22

Today, I will live within the happiness of self. Today, I will put that which is internal over that which is external. Today, I will not chase material riches. Today, I will live from the inside out. Today, good morals are the real riches I must chase!

# Day 23

Today, I know that life is not about having everything I won't but receiving all that I need. Today, I know that which the creator gives me no one can take away and that which the creator Don't want me to have no one can give me. Today, I will put my life in the creator of all creations hand!

# Day 24

Today, I will be a people's person a person of P.E.A.C.E. Properly Educating A Collective Environment while utilizing my L.I.F.E. Living Intelligently For Ever because no one else will do for me the things that I will do for myself, Today, I will be the best version of who I am!

# Day 25

Today, I will surround myself around those who have the hunger for greatness, those who realize that procrastination is the disease that can only be cured by realizing that laziness leads to procrastination. So today, I will execute the greatness that's within me!

# Day 26

Today, I want to succeed in life as bad as I want to eat when I get hungry as bad as I want to sleep when I get sleepy and tired. today, I will be like the man that runs in the rain who is preparing for a marathon in the rainforest. Today, I will not give up. Today, I will not give in. Today, I will not be scared. Today, I know that the option of failure does not exist to me. Today. I know that the only way from down is up, and I will continue to look up as I raise up!

# Day 27

Today is not about what I need in life, it's about what I don't need in life. Today, I don't need to worry about anything. Today I do not need to dwell in the past. Today I do not need to compete with no one, but myself. Today, I will, except who I am not. Today, I don't need negative energy or negative people around me. Today, I don't need to be validated by No one but myself!

# Day 28

Today, I will put God first in everything that I do. Today, I will look towards the light of God, for the light of God can see me through the darkness of the devil. Today, I will not be blind to the blessings that God has for me for the God of my understanding is that guide in my life!

# Day 29

Today, I will master myself, by realizing that time is of the essence, and I cannot get no wasted time back. Today, I will use my time to continue to be the unique and rare person that I am. Today, I know that time is limited, because time is not, and I AM for time was created by man, and I was created by the creator of all creations!

# Day 30

Today, I will not only strive for success, but I will strive to add great value to my life. Today, I will change my core thinking, as I watch my world begin to start unshrinking!

GHETTOINKPUBLICATIONS
@gmail.com

www.ingramcontent.com/pod-product-compliance
Lightning Source LLC
Chambersburg PA
CBHW060352050426
42449CB00011B/2954